C000319033

The golden age of the
Yorkshire Seaside

by Malcolm Barker

GREAT NORTHERN

GREAT NORTHERN BOOKS
Midland Chambers, 1 Wells Road, Ilkley, LS29 9JB

SUPPORTED BY
YORKSHIRE POST

© Text, Malcolm Barker 2002

Printed by Amadeus Press Ltd, Bradford

ISBN: 0-9539740-8-1

British Cataloguing in Publication Data
A catalogue for this book is available from the British Library

CONTENTS

Dedication

This book is dedicated to the men who made it possible, Yorkshire Post and Yorkshire Evening Post photographers. I spent many happy hours in the company of colleagues like Harry Fletcher, George Stott, Wilbur Wright, Peter Lowe and Irving Crawford as they humped their Speed Graphic plate cameras around the coast, intent on getting the best pictures for their newspapers.

Introduction

THE photograph on this page is from my family album, and is offered as an explanation why it was a pleasure to put together a picture book about the Yorkshire coast between the wars and into the 1960s and 70s.

The snapshot was taken by "Walking Pictures" – what we called "the happy snap men" – and the lad with mucky knees is me. Mother is hanging on to the pram firmly. too, because we were going down the steep zig-zag at Whitby, and a runaway could not be risked. Baby sister is sitting up and taking notice under her fringed sunshade.

We were on our way to a day on the beach and I was surveying the prospects, probably looking for a likely spot to build a dam. It was August 1939, so there was soon to be no more fun on the beach for five summers at least. But we had stored memories of sun, sand, sea, Mr Trillo's ice creams, Botham's lemon buns for a picnic, and Mrs Wilson's donkeys. Still they linger, more than 60 years on.

The coast and its resorts were then enjoying a Golden Age, which began after 1918. Through the 20s and 30s crowds seemed to grow every year with the introduction of holidays with pay, cheaper travel, and more white collar work. A week, or even a fortnight, at the seaside seemed everybody's idea of the perfect holiday. These happy times returned after the 1939-1945 war, but then travelling abroad in search of the sun came into fashion, and a decline in the coastal holiday trade was inevitable.

But memories remain bright, and if readers find similar happy thoughts brimming back as they turn the pages, the book will have achieved its purpose.

Malcolm Barker

Chapter 1:
Getting There

A steam passenger train negotiates one of the bends in Newtondale on the Malton to Whitby line. It was at this stage of the journey that childhood imaginings were unleashed, and the smell of the sea seemed to permeate the carriage. Oh, the sheer joy of that anticipation! The line, which was originally planned by George Stephenson as a horse railway and opened in 1836, was converted to steam, and closed on March 8th, 1965. It was revived by the North Yorkshire Moors Railway, and steam trains still ride the sinuous track, and drum across a succession of echoing bridges.

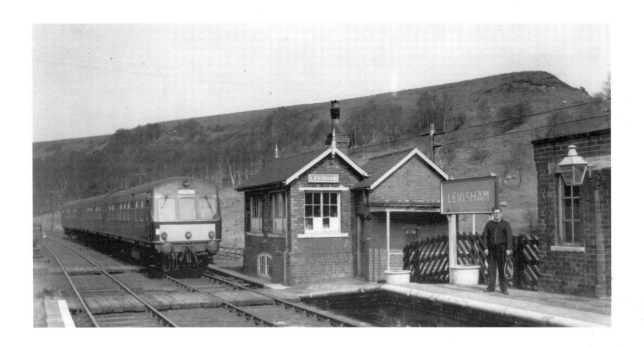

British Railways introduced diesel units on the moor line in the years before imposing closure. This one is approaching Levisham and the signalman is ready with a tablet, a safety device of a kind patented by Edward Tyer in 1878, which guarded against two trains using the same section of track.

A train crossing the valley above Staithes, on the line between Loftus and Whitby West Cliff station. In all, there were five tubular viaducts on this railway, which opened in 1883, and this was the longest (790ft) and the highest (152ft), with 17 spans. Below the track are two sections of longitudinal bracing added after the Tay Bridge disaster. The viaduct was demolished in 1960, two years after the closure of the line. Several people, including William Pybus of Whitby, then aged 80, travelled on the first train and lived to see the last.

Sir Billy Butlin (1899-1980) provided a railway station to serve his holiday camp at Filey. Among the first trains to arrive was the Yorkshire Pullman carrying 400 of his guests from King's Cross to the camp, where the San Carlo Opera Company had come straight from Covent Garden to perform La Boheme. Mr Butlin, as he was then, had persuaded the LNER to bring the Pullman back into service for the first time after the war but, alas, a fire broke out on board, resulting in a two-hour delay at Doncaster. Mr Butlin passed the time by writing personal letters of apology to his guests. Campers arriving for a holiday completed their journey on trolley trains like the one in the foreground. To judge from the character standing with his back to the fence, they were welcomed by a Town Crier complete with bell.

Happy Campers arriving for their holiday disembark on one of the station's four platforms. Although Butlin's at Filey was still attracting huge numbers in the 1970s (173,000 are said to have holidayed there in 1975) far fewer were travelling by train, and the station closed at the end of the 1977 season, five years before the camp itself was shut down.

This photograph, possibly dating from the 1920s, shows the Whitby to Pickering moor road looking towards Eller Beck, quite bereft of traffic. It is a striking reminder of how people *didn't* travel to the seaside in the early years of the 20th Century – by road!

Visitors often completed their journeys on local service buses. The Heather bus company operated services between Whitby and Robin Hood's Bay from its depot near the railway bridge immediately to the north of Bay railway station. According to a note on this Judges card, the fares in 1936 were 1s 3d return, and 11d for a child. This bus is at Fylingthorpe, at the bottom of Thorpe Bank.

There were also those wonderful charabancs. This one, with open top and solid wheels, was on an outing for the staff of Fieldings, the Bridlington photographers. Can the lady in white with a large hat really belong in the driving seat? Surely not! Perhaps the driver had got out to take the picture.

Chapter 2:

Where to Stay

The place to stay in Scarborough was for many years the Grand Hotel, designed by the architect Cuthbert Broderick for the Scarborough Cliff Hotel Company. The job was finished in 1867, but by then the hotel company had run out of funds, and money to finish the imposing structure was put up by a brave businessman. He certainly got something grand in character as well as Grand by name for his money, an astonishing edifice in brick which rose from the cliffs as if part of them, and dominated the resort with its domes and its ornate entrance. This view dates well back, but the outside appearance of the Grand, unlike the interior, has resisted change – well, grandly.

Ornate ironwork, majestic pillars and glittering chandeliers greeted guests at the Grand, as demonstrated by this photograph of the hall and staircase. The hotel set itself high standards of comfort and service, but there was perhaps some slippage after the 1939-1945 war. The Labour party held its conference in Scarborough in 1958, and Tom Driberg, the party chairman, thought it prudent to write to the manager of the Grand, where the Socialist hierarchy was booked in, requesting him not to put sauce bottles or "other vulgar condiments" on the tables. Presumably Harold Wilson (later Prime Minister and, even later, Lord Wilson of Rievaulx) had to do without his HP.

Judging by the motorcars, this view of another splendid Scarborough hotel, the Crown, was taken in the 1950s. The Crown, with its widely spaced pillars, was built in the mid-19th century as the centrepiece of the Esplanade, one of the town's architectural gems. Its design compared with that of the flamboyant Grand, conveys an air of quiet refinement. In royal terms, perhaps it is Queen Victoria to the Grand's pronouncedly male Prince Albert. In the early 21st century, it still offers the quality expected of it when it was built in 1844, and, of course, still commands the same wonderful sea-view.

CROWN HOTEL, SCARBOROUGH.

Delightful lounges

Famous for a generation, the Pavilion has comfort and charm that only long-established service can give. Its food and its cellars are known throughout the length and breadth of the country. But even more, it is known for the quiet efficiency of its homely service and the charm of its home-like surroundings. It is the headquarters of the Laughton Hotels and offers the most complete service with the largest number of permanent skilled staff in the district.

At the centre of Scarborough life, it is a headquarters for every form of enjoyment, a special attraction are the TWO HOTEL TENNIS COURTS immediately adjoining the Hotel. These constitute a delightful small holiday club, confined to the Hotel guests, with a professional in attendance.

You are strongly advised to send to Mrs. E. Laughton for the " Pavilion " Booklet, which fully describes all the amenities, including accommodation, ballroom with well-known dance band, " Norman Taylor and his Band," restaurant, grill-room, American Bar, the Hotel's own tennis courts, garage, car park, music, etc., etc.

American bar

Two splendid courts

Accommodation for 160. Running water in every bedroom. Fitted Carpets and Bedside Lights and Bells in every bedroom. Lift to all floors. Outside Iron Fire Escape Staircase. Bedrooms with private bathroom. Suites of rooms. Hotel Car Park and two Hotel Tennis Courts directly adjoining. Social and Dance Host.

Reduced wartime terms (including room, baths, four meals a day, dancing, concerts, tennis courts) from 12/- per day ; August and September from 15/- per day.

Beautiful ballroom

PAVILION HOTEL
Scarborough

Resident Director :
E. Laughton.

Telephone: 1040 (3 lines, 40 extensions). Telegrams: "Pavilion, Scarborough." A.A.****, R.A.C.

Map G. 6

The advertisement for the Pavilion Hotel at Scarborough appeared in the official Scarborough Corporation guide for 1940. The Pavilion was handy for the railway station, and run by the Laughton family, whose most famous son was Charles Laughton, the actor. The Pavilion was a splendid and welcoming place, a triumph of Victorian architecture. Its demolition in the 1960s, and replacement with a hideous concrete structure, was monstrous vandalism.

Above:
Billy Butlin chose a site on Hunmanby Moor for development and proclaimed his intention of building the biggest holiday camp in the world. Work started in 1939, but the war intervened and the first people accommodated there were servicemen, who knew the place as RAF Hunmanby Moor. It was reclaimed by its creator just 30 days after the war ended, and he was soon entertaining his first happy campers. This picture shows the camp's position in relation to the town of Filey.

Left:
Butlin's Holiday Camp near Filey was for many years the location for the greatest concentration of Yorkshire holidaymakers, famous for fun and frolics. Sixth-form girls at Whitby Grammar School, who took jobs there during the summer holidays, were considered rather daring or, as an Aunt of mine used to say somewhat sniffily, "fast". It was as near as our generation got to the Club Med. This Yorkshire Post picture, dated 1954, was taken at the height of the camp's popularity. Its fate after closure in 1983 hardly bears contemplation.

48. Camping coaches converted from Great Eastern Railway coaches were stationed at Sandsend and East Row after World War II. These are the East Row coaches, looking north, with the running line on the opposite side of the vehicles.

If hotels were too costly, there was always an old railway coach. This photograph shows old Great Eastern Railway rolling stock at Sandsend, where the camping coaches, as they were known, proved popular with holidaymakers despite the occasional clatter of a train passing on the Whitby West Cliff to Loftus line.

ABRAM 23 JAMES STREET

SMALL, NEW MODERN HOUSE.

Central for both Bays and Amusements. Board Residence, Bed and Breakfast, or Apartments. Reasonable Charges.

WELL RECOMMENDED.

Mid-day Dinner.　　Separate Tables.　　SPECIAL EASTER
AND WHITSUN TERMS.

Mrs. K. ABRAM　　　　　　　　　Map F.7

THE MOST CENTRAL POSITION IN SCARBOROUGH

ALGA HOUSE 10 ALMA SQUARE

8/6 per day Full Board. Bed and Breakfast 5/6. Alga House has H. & C. Running Water in bedrooms. Electric Light throughout and a Comfortable Lounge. Overlooking Private Gardens. Sep. Tables and Late Dinner. Car Parks and Garages near. No irksome restrictions.

For tariff apply R. CARTON.　　　　　Map G.6

ARDLUI

30 CHATSWORTH GARDENS

BOARD RESIDENCE.

ARDLUI is ideally situated.　　Adjoining Peasholm Park. 5 Minutes Sea and New Bathing Pool. Personal Supervision. H. & C. Bedrooms.　Mid-day Dinner.　Moderate Terms. Phone 2061.　　　Mrs. DOVE.　　　Map E.5

"ASH-LEIGH"

3 TRAFALGAR SQUARE

BOARD RESIDENCE.　　APARTMENTS.

Good position.　Near Peasholm Park, Floral Hall, Open-Air Theatre.　　Mid-day Dinner.　Separate Tables. H. & C. Water. Lounge. Electric Light. Terms on application.

Proprietress: Mrs. DOBSON　　　　Map E.6

Avondale Boarding House

31 BLENHEIM TERRACE

HOME COMFORTS.　　GOOD FOOD IN PLENTY. HOT AND COLD WATER in all Bedrooms.

Terms on application to:
Mrs. CRAIG and Mrs. FOWLER, Props.
Map E.8

BEULAH HOUSE

VICTORIA PARADE

Central Sunny Position.　　Convenient for Sea, Spa and All Amusements.　One minute Rail and Bus Station. BOARD RESIDENCE 7/6 BED AND BREAKFAST 4/6 Excellent Catering.　Mid-day Dinner.　Special Terms Early and Late Season. Electric Light.　Garage near. Proprietress: Mrs. J. SIMPSON　　　　Map H.6

"Beustan" 7 CARLTON TERRACE SOUTH CLIFF

Comfort with Liberal Food, daintily served, is the secret. Ideal position, overlooking delightful Gardens. 1 min. Tennis Courts, Spa and Sea. Large Lounge, Dining Room, separate Tables. Mid-day Dinner. Hot and Cold Water in Bedrooms. Electric Light. Terms: 7/6 to 8/6 per day.

Proprietors: Mrs. and Miss H. HARRISON.　　Map I.7

BLINCOLN HOUSE

69 WESTBOROUGH (Near Station).

Two Air-raid Shelters few steps from house. Nice locality. Very central, near Garages.　Clean, comfortable rooms. Special War Terms: Bed and Breakfast 28/- each.　Apartments 20/- each (no extras).　Board Residence 2 gns. each (weekly). Food will be as good and plentiful as possible under rationing conditions (hence low terms).　Single rooms extra.　Stamp, reply.

Proprietress: (Miss) S. SETTLES.　　　Map G.6

"BOGNOR"

135 QUEEN'S PARADE, NORTH BAY

Splendid position.　Sea Front. Near Tennis, Golf, Cricket, Peasholm Park,　Easy access to New Bathing Pool. Liberal Table. Highly recommended.　Wash Basins in all Bedrooms and Electric Light.　Board Residence and Apartments.　Mid-day Dinner, Lounge, etc.　Terms: Board 7/6 to 9/- per day, inclusive, according to season.　Apartments, 5/- per day. Tel. 2506　　Props.: Mr. & Mrs. N. PURDY　Map E.6

"BOWDON"

55 NORTH MARINE ROAD

BOARD RESIDENCE, BED AND BREAKFAST APARTMENTS.　Facing North Bay. HOT AND COLD WATER ALL BEDROOMS.
Separate Tables.　Mid-day Dinner.　Personal Supervision. Cosy Lounge.　Near all Entertainments.
Tel. 2449.　For Tariff apply Mrs. RHODES　Map E.7

"BRAMCOTE"

15 DEVONSHIRE DRIVE

MODERN SEMI-DETACHED VILLA.　Hot and Cold Water and Electric Light in all bedrooms.　Dining Room and comfortable lounge.　Prompt service.　Comfort assured.

TERMS:—7/6 per day to Mid-July; 8/6 per day Mid-July onwards.

Proprietress: Mrs. LOY.　　　　　Map E.5

BRIAR - DENE

38 TRAFALGAR SQUARE (late 36)

BOARD RESIDENCE.　Terms moderate.　Near Peasholm Park, Sea, Floral Hall.　Mid-day Dinner.　Separate Tables.

Electric Light.　Apartments Early and Late Season.

Proprietress: Miss CLAYTON.　　　Map E.6

BRIAR DENE

PRIVATE HOTEL, BURNISTON ROAD

STANDS IN OWN GROUNDS.　Three minutes Peasholm Park, Sands and Bathing Pool.　Bed and Breakfast if desired.　Electric Light. H. & C. Water in all Bedrooms.　Sun Parlour.　Opp. Golf Course and Open-Air Theatre. Priv. Gar. Tel. 882. Apply Tariff. Proprietresses: Mrs. MACFARLANE and Mrs. SILCOCK. Map C.4

'BRINCLIFFE EDGE'

105 QUEENS PARADE

Ideally situated, overlooking North Bay, Castle and Moors. Near New Bathing Pool, Peasholm Boating and Tennis. Hot and Cold Water in Bedrooms.
SEPARATE TABLES.　　MID-DAY DINNER. Cheerful and Homely.　　Personal Supervision.
Proprietress: Mrs. C. H. HOWKINS.　　Map E.6

Despite the outbreak of war on September 3rd 1939, Scarborough Corporation went ahead with the production of its 1940 guide, a copy of which is retained in the town's reference library. The advertisement pages make interesting reading, as this example shows. Most boarding-house keepers made a point of offering "mid-day dinner". Some thought their electric lighting worth mentioning. Few thought it necessary to adjust their announcements to take account of the war, although Miss Settles at Blincoln House did vouchsafe that "food will be good and as plentiful as possible under rationing conditions". She also offered reassurance on the availability of air raid shelters near the house.

Alexandra Hotel,

BRIDLINGTON.

Telegrams—"ALEXANDRA HOTEL, BRIDLINGTON."
Telephone—**2254**.

THE LEADING HOTEL
IN BRIDLINGTON.

Unsurpassed Situation overlooking Bay,
Flamborough Head and Private Grounds.

Nine Hole Miniature Golf Course.   Dancing.

FULLY LICENSED.

**Hot and Cold Running Water in all Bedrooms.
Open all the year round.   Heated throughout.
LIFT.**

The Alexandra Hotel had no problem justifying the claim made in this 1934 advertisement that it was Bridlington's leading hotel. Built in 1866, it was extended in 1920, and stood unchallenged for excellence and luxury until EC Briggs of Horsforth, Leeds, built the Expanse in 1937. The Alexandra was occupied by servicemen during the war, but reopened in 1949, just in time for the 1950s, a period defined by Bridlington's historians, David and Susan Neave, as the resort's "last golden decade". The hotel closed in 1975, and was subsequently demolished.

"WOODSTOCK,"
11, VERNON ROAD.

Board-Residence.
Comfortable Apartments.
One minute Sea, Tennis Courts,
Public Garage.
Near Princes Parade.
Bathing from House.
Mid-day Dinner.
Separate Tables.

Mrs. M. ROME.

ST. KITTS,
Beaconsfield, BRIDLINGTON.

Board Residence or Apartments.

Facing Tennis Courts, Garage,
and Sea. South Aspect. Central
for all amusements. Electric
Light throughout and all modern
conveniences.

Tel. 2933.

Proprietress - Mrs. HAWLEY.

LEEDS HOUSE,
40, WINDSOR CRESCENT,
BRIDLINGTON.

Board-Residence & Apartments.
One minute Sea, Spa, Station.
Electric Light throughout.
Bath. Separate Tables.
Terms—Board-res. 8/6 inclusive.
Bed and breakfast, high tea, 6/6.
Special Terms Early Season.

Mrs. M. FORD.

"The Hollies,"
78, WELLINGTON ROAD.

Board Residence.
Comfortable Apartments.
Every Convenience. Central.
Near Sea, Amusements, Station,
and Garage.
Mid-day Dinner.
Highly Recommended.
Terms Moderate.

Mrs. W. CLOSE.

"WHYNPOINT,"
19, FLAMBOROUGH ROAD,
BRIDLINGTON,

"Wins Points" for

Comfort.
Food and Service.
Cosy Lounge. Electric Light.
One minute Sea and Garage.
Board-Residence.
Bed and Breakfast.
'Phone 3321. Mrs. H. JONES.

"ZAMORA,"
11, PEMBROKE TERRACE.

Public and Private Apartments
Bed and Breakfast.
Splendid Sea View.
Near Spa, Sands and Golf Links.
Running Water in all Bedrooms.

Mrs. M. BEALE.

"ULSTERVILLE,"
3, THE CRESCENT

(Late 2, Victoria Terrace).
Overlooking Parade and Bay.
All Front Bedrooms.
Electric Light throughout.
Every Comfort.
Personal Supervision.
Public and Private Apartments or
Board. Stamp for Terms.

(Mrs.) B. McMURRAY.

C.S. and S.H.A.

21, Pembroke Terrace

APARTMENTS.
BED AND BREAKFAST.
BOARD RESIDENCE.
Mid-day Dinners.
Full Sea View.
Electric Light throughout.
Excellent Cuisine.
Liberal Table.
Bathroom. H. and C. Water

Mrs. E. A. Sadler.

A page from the 1931 guide shows a range of boarding houses available at Bridlington. Bed and breakfast with high tea at Leeds House sounds a bargain at 6s 6d (32½p) per day, but bath is offered in the singular. Perhaps there was only one?

Chapter 3:
On the Sands

Occasionally a memorable summer comes along, and it lives long in the minds of those who endure the wet years in between. The summer of 1947 was one to remember, and so was 1976 when this remarkable picture was taken at Scarborough. People crowded on the beach like bees in a swarm, and there was not much room for sand-castle building.

What a difference the sun makes! This picture, like the last, was taken at Scarborough, but the only people sitting in deckchairs, huddled against the elements, are the donkeys' minders. The animals themselves seem to be making the most of time off, and are applying themselves to their nosebags. Two other disconsolate groups can be seen nearer to harbour, and to the extreme left, stacks of deckchairs await the return of the sun.

Scarborough is basking in the sunshine again, and there is another big crowd. This picture is dated 1957, and less flesh is being exposed than in 1976. Dad, on the extreme right, has rolled up his sleeves and taken off his jacket, but it looks as though he is still in his suit trousers and waistcoat.

More sun-worshipping – at Bridlington …

...and at Filey.

Above:

This picture, taken at Scarborough in 1924, is intriguing. The women, decent in their dark costumes and swimming caps, look to be paired off for a dance. Could they have been about to attempt an early form of synchronised swimming? The lad on the left looks anxious to join the belles, and who can blame him?

Below:

A family has set itself up nicely on the sands at Scarborough. The elders relax in deckchairs in front of the bathing tent. Perhaps father, in the centre, is only resting his eyes. The children were probably very proud of their castle, and have given it a name, Rockville.

Looking across Scarborough's South Bay, with, in the foreground, the pedestrian bridge linking the town with the Spa. This was built in 1827/8, using local stone and ironwork brought from Bradford. The beach seems thinly populated, so perhaps the view was taken early in the day.

A quiet day on the promenade at Filey, dated in the early 1960s.

Bridlington, North Parade.

A crowd gathered at Bridlington looks as though it is waiting for something to happen – the tide to go out, perhaps? Whatever it is, the man on the extreme right seems to have become tired of waiting.

The sheer joy of a seaside holiday is conveyed by the smiles on the faces of these youngsters splashing about in the shallows at Whitby.

Left:
A sister of my maternal grandfather, Aunt Fanny, also at Whitby, took her pleasure far less boisterously, and is relaxing in a deck chair in what looks likes Sunday best. Her high-crowned hat will save her from too much sun, and her sensible shoes remain firmly on her feet. Alas, she may soon have to raise them, for if family tradition is correct, immediately after this photograph was taken a large and impious wave swept up the beach and surrounded her.

Below:
What Aunt Fanny might have enjoyed was a cup of tea in one of the huts lined up like a row of small terrace houses on the beach promenade. Whitby families were in the habit of taking one for the season, and usually had a kettle on the Primus. This photograph appeared in a Horne's Guide of the early 1970s, and was captioned "nearly high water", presumably to indicate there was usually more beach available.

This picture of the tram lift and pier at Saltburn is undated, but the pier appears to be intact, which was hardly its permanent condition. Soon after its opening in 1869, it was damaged by the North Sea, and even worse befell in 1924 when a sailing vessel, the Ovenbeg, was driven right through, splitting the pier in two. A repair was short-lived, because Royal Engineers reopened the gap as a precaution against invasion during the 1939-45 war. The restored pier suffered further storm damage, and the local council wanted to demolish the structure in 1975. However, amid a ferment of local opposition, the pier was saved, and has been put to rights once again.

Chapter 4:
Harbourside

The herring arrived off the Yorkshire coast during August, and proved a great attraction for holidaymakers, especially in a morning when the boats were discharging their catches. Herring were plentiful post-war, for they had not been fished intensively during 1939-45. Sometimes the market was glutted. Surplus fish were then either dumped or sent for animal feedstuffs or fertiliser. Scottish keelboats, distinguished by their varnished hulls, joined the chase, and the excitement was palpable as buyers arrived at Scarborough and Whitby with fleets of flat-topped lorries to carry the boxed fish away. There seemed to be herring for all. In Whitby, for example, a good fry was to be had on Downdinner Hill, where heavily laden lorries labouring up in first gear spilled fish across the highway. At the height of the season as many as 130 boats fished out of Whitby, and, as this picture by Doran Bros from the Whitby Literary and Philosophical Society collection shows, the harbour was crowded. One day in the 1950s, Mrs Ann Leadley, a member of a Whitby fishing family, carried piping hot Yorkshire pudding and a jug of gravy to relations on the other side, stepping from boat to boat right across the harbour.

The hunt is on for Yorkshire's silver darlings

By T. G. BARKER

THE Yorkshire coast herring fishing season is in full swing. From Scarborough and Whitby every evening except Saturdays, English and Scottish herring fishing boats are putting to sea.

The majority of the vessels use drift net fishing methods, working as individual units, but there are some which work in pairs, using ring net.

The object is the same, to catch as many fish as possible, and to get back to port early enough to catch the opening of the market when prices are at their best.

Lasting memory

The departure of the herring fishing fleet is an occasion which provides thousands of holiday makers with a memory which far outlasts anything else they recall about their holidays.

At Whitby, the recently opened West Pier extension and harbourside are always crowded as the fishermen start preparations for departure.

Nets which had been repaired and stowed away are given a final run over, the galley fire is lit to send a smoke haze rising over the evening scene in the harbour, and very often there are visitors, all warmly clad, searching for the vessel on which they are to be allowed the privilege of seeing how the nocturnal fishing of the fleet is carried out.

Suddenly one boat slips her moorings, and makes her way down stream towards the open sea. This is not prearranged—any boat can start the departure—but as soon as the fishing craft is gliding down the harbour, the odds are that there will be an immediate speed up on board others, and the night departure becomes general.

The next half-hour is the most exciting for the onlookers, and from the Extension end there are hand waving and shouted good wishes as the vessels meet the roll of the open sea and travel, quite quickly, towards Whitby Rock Buoy.

Impressive

Masthead lights flash on and the 30 to 50 fishing boats, strung out, present a most impressive sight. Crowds watch until darkness falls and then go home, a few determined to see the end of the story by rising early in the morning to see the fleet return, others to wait another night to see the same scene once more.

Yet the night viewing is not over, especially just now, when the herrings are swimming almost straight off Whitby People who leave their boardinghouses, hotels and flatlets for an evening stroll along the West Cliff see strung out for a long distance the lights of the fishing fleet, now augmented by the craft from Scarborough, Hartlepool and fleets operating in the North Sea from Holland, Poland and East Germany.

The darkness is too intense for any outline of the boats to be seen, but the lights are everywhere, and it is not unknown for strangers to Whitby to leave the Spa and wonder what town lights they can see over the sea! Some have even to be convinced that all the lights are those of herring fishing vessels.

The knowledgeable man can distinguish between the lights of drifters and ring netters and he may be able to give a clue as to whether the herrings are swimming and being caught.

The best way to follow the story of the fishing is to listen in on the trawler radio band, when it is highly probable that some radio operator on coastal cargo vessels will have something to say about the lights of " The City of Edinburgh."

A Yorkshire Post report of 1960 from its Whitby correspondent (my father was also editor of the Whitby Gazette), gives the herring the name used by fishermen, "Silver Darlings". This referred not merely to their shiny scales, but also to the financial benefits they conferred on the fisherfolk. There were profits, too for those in the holiday trade, for the spectacle of the fleet putting to sea was a great draw, and holidaymakers were kept informed of the time of sailing by notices chalked daily on a board.

Scarborough was an old-established herring fishing port, and was accustomed to "foreigners" joining in the bonanza, including Cornishmen before the First World War, and fishermen from Yarmouth and Lowestoft between the wars. From 1946, it was the turn of the Scots. The vessel in the foreground was from Fraserburgh. Others came from small ports like Peterhead, Banff, and Lossiemouth. Some were operated by "Wee Frees", notable for strict religious observance, including a refusal to sail on the Sabbath.

A huge catch, with the hold of the keelboat full to brimming, is being hoisted ashore by basket, a laborious task. Fish were caught by drift netting, or, more frequently, ring netting with two boats working together to encircle a shoal. Herring might have survived this depredation, but the introduction of the catch-all Norwegian purse seine net cleared them from the sea, 1.2m tonnes in 1965 alone. Suddenly, the North Sea herring fishery, which had survived since man first cast a net in the ocean, was no more.

There was another fine catch for fishermen during the summer – holidaymakers. The owners of these Bridlington cobles seem to be having a rich haul on a summer's day. To modern eyes, the trippers seem to have dressed up for the occasion, notably the couple facing the camera in the left foreground, second boat along. They are plainly aware of the camera, and are displaying admirably stiff upper lips.

The coal-powered Yorkshireman, an old favourite with holidaymakers, lies alongside during a busy day at Bridlington (note the crowd gathered on the pier to the left) while a fishing boat on pleasure bent, the Britannia, heads for the harbour mouth. Her passengers look to be packed as close as, well, herrings in a hold.

Bridlington harbour from aloft, a picture taken at Eastertide in 1960, and doesn't the town look busy?

Not only does Boy's Own float, but so does its apostrophe. But that would not worry the sailor in the bows, because he can rejoice in a full complement of passengers on this Whit Sunday in 1961, and nearly all of them obliged Wilbur Wright, the Yorkshire Post photographer based at Hull, with wide and happy smiles. Some even waved.

Another crowded pleasure boat in Bridlington, the Yorkshire Belle this time, offered a cruise for half a crown (12½p).

Left:

This picture helped clear a mystery that baffled some people on the Yorkshire coast in the years after the 1939-45 war. It seemed to them that the man they knew as Professor Twigg, who arrived as if from nowhere during the holiday season, and enthralled visitors with various aquatic feats, had the secret of eternal youth, for he had the same name and appearance as a man who had put on similar shows in the years after the Great War. In fact there were two Professors Twigg, father and son, seen here posing together in near-identical costumes. Off-season, they worked as miners in the West Riding, and kept in trim at Featherstone Baths. The father, Bill Twigg, who performed at Bridlington in company with a Prof Grotier, died in 1955. His son, Billy, died in 1973.

Left:
Prof Twigg the Younger, who seems ready to perform his feat of smoking underwater, is seen here on Whitby pier, together with William "Spot" Gale (left) and a Whitby man tentatively identified as Arthur Pearson who used the megaphone to announce the Professor's programme from Scotch Head. Bellowed announcements such as "Professor Twigg will now give his impression of a dolly tub" soon drew the crowds, and they were not disappointed. There were imitations of a porpoise and a submarine, an underwater escape from handcuffs, and then the astonishing business with the cigarette from which the Professor puffed smoke after a long immersion.

Above:
Coronia is a name to conjure with on the Yorkshire coast, for a pleasure boat of that name distinguished herself and earned honour for her crew by taking part in the evacuation of Dunkirk. This may be the very vessel, but the Yorkshire Post library has put a note of warning on the back of the print: "Do not confuse with old Coronia".

Chapter 5:
What shall we do?

Holidaymaking fathers often escaped a day on the beach by going to the cricket. Scarborough's first-class games, culminating in the Festival at the end of the season, drew large crowds. This postcard shows the Yorkshire side which played a three-day game against Warwickshire in August 1949, the season when Yorkshire shared the Championship with Middlesex.

Len Hutton (later Sir Leonard) and Frank Lowson opened the innings for Yorkshire. This was perhaps staged, for spectators are still wandering around the pitch, a happy tradition at Scarborough.

YORKSHIRE COUNTY CRICKET CLUB
SCARBOROUGH CRICKET GROUND
YORKSHIRE v WARWICKSHIRE
on August 17th. 18th. & 19th. 1949

WARWICKSHIRE	First Innings		Second Innings	
1 J. R. THOMPSON	b Coxon...	7	Hbw. b Coxon c Close	24
2 F. C. Gardner	lbw Close	17	lbw Coxon	2
3 A. Townsend	c Close b Coxon	39	c Brennan b Close	26
4 J. S. Ord	run out	51	lbw Close	0
5 H. E. Dollery (Capt.)	c Hutton b Coxon	42	lbw Wardle	16
6 A. V. Wolton	c Hutton b Foord	4	b Foord	8
7 A. H. Kardar	c Brennan b Close	35	b Wardle	22
8 R. T. Spooner	not out	32	c Brennan b Close	4
9 C. W. Grove	c Coxon b Foord	1	c Lowson b Wardle	4
10 T. L. Pritchard	c Brennan b Foord	9	c Lester b Coxon	4
11 W. E. Hollies	c Hutton b Foord	1	not out	0
	b 2 lb 5 w... nb...	7	b 2 lb 6 w 2 nb 1.	11
	Total	245	Total	171

Fall of the Wickets

1	2	3	4	5	6	7	8	9	10	1	2	3	4	5	6	7	8	9	10
11 ...	...																		

ANALYSIS of BOWLING

	First Innings Overs	Mdns.	Runs	Wkts.	Second Innings Overs	Mdns.	Runs	Wkts.
Coxon	32	10	59	3	26.5	9	55	3
Foord	30.1	5	77	4	16	5	30	1
Close	23	9	51	2	17	6	27	3
Yardley	4	0	12	0	26	11	48	3
Wardle	19	7	39	0				

YORKSHIRE	First Innings		Second Innings	
1 L. Hutton	b Grove	47		
2 F. A. Lowson	lbw Pritchard	0		
3 W. Watson	b Pritchard	115		
4 E. Lester	lbw Grove	86		
5 J. V. Wilson	c Spooner b Hollies	71		
6 N. W. D. Yardley (Capt.)	c Kardar b Townsend	28		
7 D. B. Close	run out			
8 A. Coxon	not out	17		
9 J. H. Wardle	b Grove	0		
10 D. V. Brennan	not out	5		
11 C. W. Foord	d. n. b			
	b... lb... w... nb...		b... lb... w... nb...	—
(8 wkts. dec)	Total	484	Total	...

Fall of the Wickets

1	2	3	4	5	6	7	8	9	10	1	2	3	4	5	6	7	8	9	10
...	...	...																	

ANALYSIS of BOWLING

	First Innings Overs	Mdns.	Runs	Wkts.	Second Innings Overs	Mdns.	Runs	Wkts.
Pritchard	32	1	120	2	...	...	...	...
Grove	39.6	6	96	3	...	...	...	...
Hollies	39	13	107	1	...	...	...	...
Kardar	29	4	104	1	...	...	...	...
Townsend	13	1	47	1				
Ord	4	2	3	0				

Hours of play :- Wed. 11-30 to 7   Thurs. 11 to 7   Friday 11 to 4

New Ball Rule :- White Disc shown at 55th over; Yellow Disc shown at 60th over; White & Yellow Discs 65th, after which new ball may be taken

WRIGHT & CO., LTD., North Street, SCARBOROUGH.

A special treat for Yorkshire fans who indulge in nostalgia – the complete match card. It was probably sold by Arthur Smith, who followed Yorkshire with his memorable cry: "I have all the batters in the order of going in." This card would be printed at the ground, and by the time it went to press Yorkshire already had a wicket, Warwickshire's opener clean-bowled by Alec Coxon, who went on to take more than 100 wickets that season. His run-in did not vary. A memory of that match is Alec Coxon's spoor, a line of footsteps imprinted in the grass, beginning towards the boundary and ending at the wicket. Yorkshire won the match by an innings on the third day.

Above:
If there was no cricket to divert Dad, there was always the model railway. The miniature locomotive, Neptune, is numbered 1932, the year of its purchase. It may resemble one of Sir Nigel Gresley's magnificent Pacifics, but like its partner, Triton (No. 1931 – the year the railway opened), the locomotive was provided with diesel power from the start. The railway was not trouble-free. There were head-on collisions, the first in 1932, and derailments in 1957 and 1960.

Right:
By 1936, the date on this postcard, Whitby Spa Band had matured into Frank Gomez and the Municipal Orchestra, of sufficient calibre to be broadcast by the BBC, as was happening here, under the Spa Pavilion's glass roof.

Above:

Music-making was an integral part of the entertainment at all resorts. This group, posing in the 1920s with their instruments among assorted herbage, is identified on the reverse of the photograph as "Whitby Spa Band". One player in the band before 1914 was GWJ Potter, who lived at Woodford, Essex. He used his spare time to write A History of the Whitby and Pickering Railway, now an admired and sought-after book.

Scarborough, too, had a tradition for providing good light
classical music, and the grandeur of the setting on the Spa
is conveyed by this photograph, taken in the1960s.
The variety on offer in, say, 1962 was remarkable –
The Fol-de-Rols at the Floral Hall, Max Jaffa at the Spa
Grand Hall, and Hedley Ward and his band in the
Spa Ballroom.

Max Jaffa, whose name became inextricably linked with music-making in Scarborough.

Until the 1980s, the Yorkshire Evening Post ballroom
dancing competition was a staple of the season at
Bridlington, drawing couples from far and wide for the
weekly heats and culminating in a grand final in
September danced for many years to Edwin Harper and
his music. Peter Lowe's picture shows contestants
parading in 1980 for the final's curtain-raiser, an
attractive dress competition, when sequins twinkled as
plenteously as stars in the Milky Way.

A display by professionals was part of the final night. Here Michael and Vicki Barr, the British Professional Modern Dance champions in 1980, draw applause from a knowledgeable crowd.

Open Air Theatre, Pleasure Park, Scarborough.

Above:

Golfers on the North Cliff course at Scarborough commented on the remarkable acoustic properties of an area around Burniston Road and thus, in 1932, an astonishing enterprise was launched, The Open-Air Theatre. The former Borough engineer, Harry Smith, in the words of one enthusiast, created the 8,000-seater arena, shown on this postcard, from a wasteland during the depressed 1930s. The town's Amateur Operatic Society responded to the challenge with Merrie England in 1932, and went from success to success, Faust, Carmen, Tannhauser, and then, with the war over, back to Merrie England in 1945. The last in the post-war sequence of productions was West Side Story in 1968

Above:
In 1965 the Scarborough Operatic Society presented an
ambitious open-air performance of The King and I. Here
Anna, played by Jean Barrington, is seen landing
in Bangkok.

Left:
Rose Marie was put on in 1962 and enjoyed a successful
12-week run. Audiences at the "biggest open-air theatre
in Europe", a claim verified by the Guinness Book of
Records, brought rugs and hot drinks in vacuum flasks.
Coach outings were arranged from neighbouring resorts,
the West Riding and the Northeast.
As usual, there was a strong professional contribution to
Rose Marie, and the producer/director, Robinson Cleaver,
and leading cast members of the 1962 show autographed
the back of a postcard.

The new North Bay bathing pool at Scarborough shown
in 1939, when it first opened.

A post-war view of a great crowd at the South Bay pool at Scarborough.

Chapter 6:
Bygones

Visiting Scarborough's Gala-land, originally opened in 1877 as an extremely grand aquarium, was like descending into another world. The entrance, almost directly below Cliff Bridge, led into an Indo-Moorish underworld, an exotic creation of the architect Eugenius Birch. Pillars richly painted in red supported equally gaudy Byzantine arches, a veritable People's Palace. Amid the intermittent roar of the ghost train, the ping-pinging from shooting galleries and the cries of bingo-callers could sometimes be heard the genteel strains of an orchestra as Thelma Hammond's all-girls' band played bravely on.

In the years immediately after the war, Gala Land featured slot machines, which, in return for a penny, offered enactments of such events as an execution, or the drunkard's return home. These were clockwork wonders, and young audiences flocked round, their noses pressed to the glass cases within which the various scenes were acted out. This picture shows the prosaic entrance to the delights below.

PEOPLE'S PALACE AND

AQUARIUM

SCARBOROUGH.

The most Magnificent Underground Palace in the World. Nearly 3 acres of Superb Indian
Architecture.
Not a dull moment from opening to closing. A Cool Retreat in Hot Weather.
10 Hours' continuous round of Varied Entertainments.
Open Daily, 9 a.m. to 11 p.m. Sundays, 1 to 10 p.m.

Admission (including all Entertainments) **Sixpence.**
Season Tickets, 10s. 6d. Monthly do., 5s. Weekly do., 2s. 6d.

Great Attractions for the Season.

Splendid New Scenery and Act Drop for Indian Theatre, specially painted by the eminent
Scenic Artiste, Mr. W. Phillips.

VOORZANGER'S COSMOPOLITAN

Ladies' & Gentlemen's Orchestra

21 in number, including Eminent Soloists, will give a

GRAND CONCERT every SUNDAY at 8.

MONDAY, AUGUST 27th, and during the Week,

CONCERTS DAILY at 12 noon, 3, and 7-30.

Grand Orchestra & Vocalists.

Swimming Exhibitions

In Large Swimming Bath by Miss Ada Webb and Troupe of Lady Swimmers
and High Divers, at Intervals.

Re-engagement for One Week Only of

UNTHAN,

The Armless Wonder, who Plays Violin, Cornet, Fires Gun with his Feet, Plays Cards, &c.
The Marvel of the Age.

MISS FLO EVERETTE,

And her Clever Canine Pets, introducing Somersaults, Serpentine Dancing, Leaping, &c.

MR. WALTER WADE,

The Favorite Humorist and Lady Impersonator. "The Male Patti."

HARRY MARS, Tramp Gymnast.

Last Week of the Original **FOUR M.P.'S.**
(The MUSICAL PALMERS, F.O.S.. C.D.D.),
In their Military Musical Speciality, "Lively After Parade," introducing an entirely
New Fantasia for Bugles and Drums, giving the calls of the British Army Regiments in
South Africa, and on their Silver Quartette a Grand Selection of Popular Melodies.

Important Engagement of

CYRUS & MAUDE,

Musical Comedians, also their Live Performing Donkey, "BESS." Everyone should see the
Burlesque of "Dick Turpin's Ride to York," as played by Cyrus and his Donkey.
Came, Forth, With.

LITTLE DAISY PALMER,

The Celebrated Juvenile Song and Dance Artiste.

ZASMA, Acrobat.

PROF. DEVONO, Conjuror, with New Tricks, &c.

And Other Artistes.

Two Baby Bears will promenade the building at Intervals.
The Monkey House and Aviary.—New Additions, including 2 Baby Bears. Seal
Ponds (Seals are fed at 10-30, 2-10, and 8-45.) Illuminated Tanks, Grottoes, Caves,
Cosmoramic Views, Camera Obscura, &c.
Dancing in the Ball Room without extra charge. Full Band.
M.C., Prof. Cunningham.

All Free for the Gate Admission of Sixpence.

BLAKE'S DIOGRAPH,

A Series of Animated Pictures, including the entire Story of "Cinderella," and the Latest

WAR PICTURES

Straight from the Battlefield of South Africa. See the Latest Picture, Her Majesty's Visit
to Ireland. Grand Review in Phoenix Park, Dublin. See Pictures from Modder River
and Magersfontein, also our Favourites at the Front.
New Stereoscopic Room, 36 Views, with War Pictures.
Swimming Bath open to the Public for Bathing Daily, 7 to 10-30 a.m.,
5-30 to 8 and 9-15 to 10 p.m. Tuesdays and Fridays, 9 to 11 a.m., for Ladies only.
Sundays, 7 to 10-30 a.m. Lessons given in Swimming. For terms apply to the Manager.
EVERY MONDAY.—GRAND ILLUMINATED GALA. Thousands of Colored
Lights, Devices, and Transparencies.
W. MORGAN, Managing Director.

MARSHALL & SON, PRINTERS.

An advertisement from the early days of the 20th Century showing the kind of entertainment offered by the "People's Palace and Aquarium". As well as Harry Marr, "the tramp gymnast" and Unthan, "the armless wonder, who plays violin, cornet, fires gun with his feet", there was Blake's Diograph with Boer War pictures "straight from the battlefield."

GALA LAND

SCARBOROUGH'S BRIGHTEST SPOT
11 a.m. ● 11 p.m.
MELODY, MIRTH and MERRIMENT

EVELYN HARDY AND HER ALL BRITISH Ladies Band
England's Premier Lady Cornettist.   The Musical Sensation of the Season.
PLAYS DAILY, Mornings, Afternoons and Evenings, in the WINTER GARDENS with its WONDERFUL ILLUMINATED FOUNTAINS and FLORAL BEAUTY.

DECAR'S CIRCUS PERFORMING MONKEYS, GEESE and PONIES. CYCLON, The Kicking Mule.

CHUNG LING SEN and Company. ORIENTAL MYSTIC PHANTASY.

MADAM JEAN,   PROF. FREDERICK
CLAIRVOYANT.   AND HIS MOUSE CIRCUS.

RESTAURANT CAFÉ. DAINTY TEAS, HOT SUPPERS, CREAM ICES. ALL AT MODERATE PRICES.

Admission to Gala Land 4d. ; Children 2d.   ALL THE FUN OF THE FAIR

Gala-land was acquired by Scarborough Corporation after the First World War and this advertisement shows the variety of entertainment available there in the 1930s.

Sadly, Gala-land lost its appeal, and Scarborough decided to turn it into an underground car-park. A crowd watches from the Cliff Bridge as the old arches are laid bare during the process of demolition in 1968.

Left:

Tin Ghaut (or, as this Valentine card has it, Tin Ghant!) was a picturesque corner of old Whitby until the Urban Council did away with it, and used the site for car-parking. The charming appearance of the ginnel sloping down to the upper harbour among old cottages appealed greatly to artists and photographers. But the reality was squalor, for Tin Ghaut was an unsanitary slum, with no running water in the homes (note the communal tap at the foot of the building on the right). Even so, it would probably have been modernised and preserved today.

Below:

Whitby Urban Council seems to have been proud of its achievement in destroying much of the old town. In Horne's Guide in the early 70s, contrasting pictures were provided to demonstrate how the old galleried houses on Boulby Bank, on the east side above Church Street, had been ripped down and replaced with dreadfully dull flats.

NEW COUNCIL FLATS ON BOULBY BANK, CHURCH STREET
(which replace the old style galleried houses—now demolished)

Chapter 7:
Among the locals

Mary Ann Pennock, in a long black dress, a bonnet, and shawl, was once a familiar figure in Whitby, where she gathered periwinkles on the shore. She had her moment of national fame when she sought to confound the likes of Gilbert Harding and Isobel Barnett on the BBC TV programme, "What's My Line", with her occupation as a winkle gatherer. She worked for upwards of 80 years, and could recall picking oakum used for caulking the seams of wooden sailing ships. Mary Ann died in 1958, aged 94. Right to the end of her life, she walked the shore daily, often with as many as six of her cats in attendance. She married comparatively late in life and was known in the town as "Mary Ann Akkie".

Two wearers of Staithes bonnets, identified as Miss Dalton and Mrs Clarke, posed for this photograph at Runswick Bay in 1950. At one time each coastal township had its bonnet in much the same way as each had a local pattern for fishermen's guernseys. The bonnets had a good practical use, for they afforded protection when the fisherwomen balanced heavy baskets of mussels on their heads as they took them home for use as bait. Then, when the lines were baited, the women coiled them tightly on to a flat wooden basket, which they carried on their heads down to the boats. In such circumstances, headgear that protected the shoulders and nape of the neck was a practical necessity, and it was the genius of the womenfolk to make them attractive as well. Staithes bonnets, which are still being made, require a yard of cotton material, a yard of cotton tape, and a piece of wadding used for quilting at the front.

Another face full of character here in a Frank Meadow Sutcliffe study, which he turned into a postcard, and called "Peace". The elderly woman, who, sadly, has not been identified, is wearing a traditional bonnet, and sits patiently at her darning.

A trio of fishermen relaxing at the harbour side at
Scarborough in the 1950s. The man in the centre is
wearing a guernsey of traditional design.

A team of "climmers", as the harvesters of gulls' eggs from the East Riding chalk cliffs in the Flamborough area were known. The leader was Bob Hartley (second from the left) and the others were (l to r) Arthur Edmond, Alf Corner and Bill Prince. The collection called for skill and daring, and continued long after the avian colonies had come under the protection of the Sea Birds Preservation Act, which was promoted by a local MP, Christopher Sykes, and became law in 1869. The Protection of Birds Act, 1954, eventually outlawed egg-collecting. Between the wars, it was rated a holiday attraction, and the Ward Lock guide to Filey from that era reported that the season was at its height in May and the beginning of June, "but there is often plenty to see even in July".

A jolly trio of waitresses posing outside a Bridlington
café in the 1920s. The offer of Devonshire ice-cream is a
variation on the more prevalent offering of Devonshire
cream teas.

Who has not rejoiced over a delicious East coast crab? Filey's Frank Jenkinson was probably emphasising the freshness of the wares on offer when he added the word fisherman in parenthesis after his name. It offered a guarantee, straight from sea to stall. On this old picture, his brother Jim has been left in charge, and is taking a cigarette break

Chapter 8:
A trip down the Coast

THE Yorkshire coast and its hinterland offers great variety, not least in the character of its cliffs, massive at Boulby, abrupt at Bempton, and fading to the diminutive on the Holderness shore. Following its course from Teesmouth to the Humber, with occasional ventures inland, is a rewarding experience.

The journey begins at Redcar, which may not be in the first rank as a resort nowadays, but aspired to join the emerging watering places in the mid-19th Century. A Visitors' Guide reached its second edition in 1852, and a contribution attributed to "a surgeon" assured readers that "as a general stimulant, as a restorer of nervous energy, Sea Air possesses powers and properties superior to any other". No doubt this wonderful stuff was freely available in ample quantities on Redcar's pier, shown in this picture of 1896. Redcar also has a fine beach, eight miles of firm sand

Above:

Henry Pease, one of those wonderful Victorians who had dreams and made them happen, created modern Saltburn. The Stockton and Darlington Railway, in which his family's company, Pease and Partners had a substantial interest, extended its line there, and in 1859, Henry Pease set up the Saltburn Improvement Company. In 1863, the Zetland Hotel, was opened, a "princely pile" as someone called it at the time, to an Italianate design. As required of other buildings in Saltburn, its frontage complied with the general requirement in the town, and was finished in white firebrick (manufacturers: Peace West Brickworks in Co Durham). A special platform extended the railway to the back door. British Railways closed this extension in 1970. By then, the Zetland had fallen on hard times, and the writer of this note had the eerie experience of being the only guest there one night in the late 1960s.

Left:

This picture is included to demonstrate the sheer style which Henry Peace brought to Saltburn. Who has ever seen such a water tower? It might almost have strayed to Lune Street, Saltburn, from Morocco. Alas, it did not work very well, and was eventually demolished, its quota of white firebricks being used to build a row of houses, known locally as Water Tower Terrace.

Above:

The Cod and Lobster inn at Staithes occupies a vulnerable position when the North Sea runs wild. It is, however, a popular watering place, even though John Howard in his admirable history, Staithes, which he published in 2000, suggests that it might once have provided accommodation for the dreaded Revenue Officers. The village was notorious for its smugglers in the 18th Century

Below:

A venture inland to the village of Beckhole, and an unusual viewpoint for Harry Fletcher's camera presented itself partway up the bank ascending from the village to the railway bridge and Green End. The Birch Tree inn can just be glimpsed on the extreme left. At the time of the picture (1967) it was kept by Mrs Schofield who, in addition to fine ales, served delicious free-range eggs, boiled to perfection, in her tearoom upstairs.

This delightful view of Runswick Bay pre-dates the prettification of the village. Flights of worn stone steps lead up to the cottages and opposite them, to the left of the picture, is a structure that may be a wooden privy. In 1907 the Leeds Mercury, a predecessor of the Yorkshire Post, recorded the results of a readers' poll to determine the prettiest place in Yorkshire (Thornton-le-Dale was a runaway winner with 11,111 votes). Runswick Bay ranked only 18th in readers' assessments, but still occupied first place among the coastal haunts, beating both Robin Hood's Bay (24th) and Sandsend (36th).

The Spa, Whitby.

Above:
The handsome Whitby Spa Pavilion now swept away in favour of a monstrosity with all the charm of a pillbox.

Below:
Bathing tents in place on the sands below Whitby West Cliff. Interest is added by the work going on at the end of the piers, where the extensions appear to be nearing completion. This is therefore a pre-First World War picture.

This is an old picture, probably late Victorian, taken by the Whitby district photographer Tom Watson, who was a contemporary of Frank Meadow Sutcliffe. The tide is in and the Argument family's bathing machines have been parked at the bottom of Khyber Pass for safety. This family lent its name to Argument's Yard off Church Street. There is, therefore, no implication in the title of a tendency to fractiousness among the yard's inhabitants. Even so, the Arguments' bequest is the town's most photographed, coveted, and stolen nameplate.

Robin Hood's Bay, possibly in the early 1920s, and nothing seems to have changed a great deal since then. Even the smooth boulders, arranged to protect the bridge parapet (right) from the wheels of carts are still in place.

Robin Hood's Bay again, with cobles drawn up on the landing at Bayfoot. A Robin Hood's Bay historian, Barrie Farnill, used to assert there was no better view in the world than that commanded from the men's lavatory at the Bay Hotel. Barrie recorded in Robin Hood's Bay (Dalesman, 1966) that an earlier inn was washed away by a high tide in 1843, and the bowsprit of a wrecked merchantman once crashed through a window of the replacement building.

THE CLIFFS, RAVENSCAR, 250

This card, dated 1929, shows the steps connecting the Raven Hall Hotel on its headland near Robin Hood's Bay with the shore below. The writer, identified only as Dave, sent it to his mother at the School House, Sheriff Hutton, and exclaimed over the height of the cliffs. Looking from them down to the sea, "the small waves look just as though someone was blowing into a bowl of water and making model boats go round the head". On a more earthy plane, Dave confides he is hungry ("I feel like an empty vacuum"), but all should soon have been well, for "Mollie is now cooking bacon".

The magnificent Rotunda at Scarborough was built in 1828-29 for the Scarborough Philosophical Society. Its circular design was suggested by William Smith, "The Father of English Geology", as the best means to demonstrate the stratifications of the rocks of the British Isles. Smith was steward to Sir John Johnstone of Hackness, who was first president of the Philosophical Society and a prime mover in the building of the Rotunda, now an admirable museum.

One of the delights of Scarborough is the existence of quiet corners, often no great distance from more garish and clamourous attractions. These gardens, at St Nicholas Cliff, where footpaths zigzag on a steep slope, are a good example.

Old favourites with holidaymakers were the two grand Ladies of the coast, the Yorkshire Lady and the Regal Lady, which were operated by a firm called Scarborough Cruises Ltd. Here, on a Bank Holiday in 1957, Regal Lady gathers speed as she heads for open water from Scarborough harbour.

NORTH LANDING, FLAMBOROUGH

Above:

Some of the finest scenery in Yorkshire lies in the vicinity of Flamborough Head, where the chalk cliffs provide endless interest for geologists. This view of North Landing shows cobles drawn up the beach, and one entering the bay with a full complement of trippers. One of the oddities that emerge from these old photographs is the apparent lack of any kind of leisurewear. The couple in the foreground, for example, are clad as if they were on their way to church in Sunday best, with the lady in a smart belted coat and the gentleman in a dark suit. He does seem to have rolled his trousers up though, so sombre dress did not altogether preclude some frivolity.

FLORAL STAIRCASE, ROYAL PRINCES PARADE, BRIDLINGTON

Left:
Often, the messages on old postcards are as interesting as the cards themselves. This was written by Marion on 10th September 1924, to a friend in Leeds called Olive. Marion is hoping Olive can join her and promises "a posh time" She adds, "It's glorious here", which was nice for Bridlington. The card itself shows a remarkable feature in the resort's Prince's Parade called "A floral staircase". Prince's Parade was given its name in 1888 to commemorate the visit of a grandson of Queen Victoria, Prince Albert Victor, and many shared the postcard writer's enthusiasm for an area with "beautifully laid out flowerbeds, shrubberies and walks". In the 1980s, Prince's Parade became just another funfair

Above:
If Bridlington lost the pleasance of Prince's Parade, it continued to offer the glories of Sewerby Hall and gardens, acquired in 1934 by the Corporation for £45,000 from Mr Yarburgh Lloyd-Greame. This photograph was taken in the 1960s, and conveys the elegance of the extensive parkland, which surrounds the house After Sewerby's acquisition by the town, the official opening to the public was performed by the aviatrix Amy Johnson on June 1st, 1936. She is now commemorated by a museum in the hall.

An air picture of Hornsea, which promoted itself on railway posters as "Lakeland by the Sea". The resort was largely the creation of Joseph Armytage Wade (1820-1893) who brought the Hull and Hornsea Railway to the town in 1862, built an ill-fated pier, established the Hornsea Brick and Tile Works (a predecessor of the Hornsea Pottery), and generally attempted to bring prosperity to Hornsea and make himself rich in the process. The railway lasted until 1964, when it was closed under the Beeching plan.

Hornsea's wonderful natural attraction is the Mere, the largest fresh-water lake in Yorkshire, about two miles long and a mile broad. This picture was taken in 1967, and shows Swordfish class racing dinghies breezing along. In the foreground, feeding the swans, are two sisters from Bradford, Angela and Gail Garner.

Withernsea's most memorable building is the lighthouse, an elegant white structure a little inland on the Hull road. It was put up in 1892-1894, and although it ceased to function as a light in 1976, it remains in use as a museum, and its 120ft tower provides excellent views along the long flat Holderness shore.

Chapter 9:
Storm and Tempest

Mostly, holidaymakers see a quiescent North Sea, calm
except for a few breakers near the beach. But gales lash it
into a fury, as this photograph taken on Marine Drive,
Scarborough, at the height of a north-easterly blow,
amply demonstrates. Wave-dodging in conditions like
this is dangerous to the point of idiocy.

The force generated by waves is tremendous. This photograph of the old Toll House at the northern end of Marine Drive at Scarborough shows the after-effects of a storm, which has ripped off most of the roof.

The North Sea surge of February 1953, which elsewhere caused great loss of life, is also remembered with awe on the Yorkshire coast. This extraordinary picture, taken by Doran Bros from outside their shop on St Anne's Staith, Whitby, shows the harbour brimming with water at high tide, with the pier near the lifeboat house totally engulfed.

As the gale drove the surge down the North Sea in February 1953, folk ventured out to see the damage. The two women to the right probably wish they had stayed at home a little longer, for a gust is threatening to send them flying among the debris on the West Pier at Whitby.

The astonishing power of the sea is demonstrated by this photograph taken in 1953 by John Tindale on the East pier at Whitby where massive chunks of masonry have been uprooted and flung about as if they were no more substantial than tiddlywinks.

Havoc, too, at Robin Hood's Bay, where the 1953 storm wrecked the slipway and it had to be fenced off.

John Tindale also depicted devastation at Sandsend, where stone bollards were flung about like ninepins, and the sea gouged its way across the carriageway to within a yard or two of seafront properties.

Acknowledgments

IN this book, Yorkshire Post Newspapers photographs have been supplemented from the private collections of David Joy, Eric Simpson and Malcolm Barker, and from Scarborough and Bridlington Reference Libraries, the Whitby Literary and Philosophical Society, the National Railway Museum and the Ken Hoole Study Centre at Darlington. The publisher and the compiler would like to thank all who assisted, and especially Stephen Allinson, Promotions and Publicity manager at Yorkshire Post newspapers, his colleague Paul Bolton, and Sarah Collis in the Yorkshire Post library.

Great Yorkshire Books from

GREAT NORTHERN

Dales People at Work

The Great Yorkshire Celebrity Cookbook

Hannah Hauxwell: The Common-sense Book of a Countrywoman

The Two Way Guide to the Settle Line

The Tale of the Mouse

The Yorkshire Dales: A Landscape Through Time

Austin Mitchell's YORKSHIRE JOKES

Austin Mitchell's TALKIN' YORKSHER

The Wensleydale Railway

A Right Royal Occasion

Richard Whiteley's YORKSHIRE QUIZ

Other books published by Great Northern include:

Arthur Ransome and the World of the Swallows & Amazons

Farm Yarns

Sandwalker

Sand-pilot of Morecambe Bay

For further information on these or forthcoming titles please call Great Northern Books on 01943 604027.